ZEPHAN WONG

The Productivity Path

Overcome procrastination, boost productivity and master time management

Copyright © 2024 by zephan wong

All rights reserved. No part of this publication may be reproduced, stored or transmitted in any form or by any means, electronic, mechanical, photocopying, recording, scanning, or otherwise without written permission from the publisher. It is illegal to copy this book, post it to a website, or distribute it by any other means without permission.

zephan wong asserts the moral right to be identified as the author of this work.

zephan wong has no responsibility for the persistence or accuracy of URLs for external or third-party Internet Websites referred to in this publication and does not guarantee that any content on such Websites is, or will remain, accurate or appropriate.

Designations used by companies to distinguish their products are often claimed as trademarks. All brand names and product names used in this book and on its cover are trade names, service marks, trademarks and registered trademarks of their respective owners. The publishers and the book are not associated with any product or vendor mentioned in this book. None of the companies referenced within the book have endorsed the book.

First edition

This book was professionally typeset on Reedsy.
Find out more at reedsy.com

Contents

1. The Productivity Path — 1
2. How to read this book — 3
3. Timeline — 6
4. Power Hour — 9
5. To Do Priorities — 11
6. Less is More — 13
7. You Are The Average Of Your 5 Closest Friends — 15
8. The Grass is Greenest Where You Water It — 17
9. 3 Breaths — 19
10. You Are What You Eat — 21
11. Conclusion — 24
12. Resources — 25

1

The Productivity Path

Introduction

Ever wonder why we start off on a new project so excited, filled with hope and anticipation and then halfway through we lose motivation and decide to throw in the towel? Or why even though we know we absolutely need to get this piece of work done but still decide to scroll through our phones or watch TV instead? If you are as human as me, you have probably faced this scenario before and you have come to the right place to learn how to overcome there.

I'm Zephan, a student of life and have tried different productivity methods, life hacks and courses in order to find the best methods that work. Here in this short book I've distilled all of them into the absolute essentials you need to walk through a life of fulfillment where you are able to reach all your goals, dreams and desires.

When you are easy on yourself, life will be hard on you and when you are hard on yourself, life will be easy. We all know intuitively that we should walk the hard route today so that our tomorrows don't suffer, yet why do we still choose the easy route? This book is about making the hard decisions you should become the default option in your life. This will not just improve your business and work life but also every other area of health, relationships and spirituality as you choose the things that matter the most to you. Well let's jump right on this productivity path!

2

How to read this book

The most ideal way to read this book would be like a normal book, reading through it chapter by chapter. If however, you feel a certain chapter speaking to you more feel free to jump straight into it. As long as you are able to learn something new and apply it to improve your life, I am happy that this book has helped you.

I've also included actionable steps that you should take at the end of each chapter so this book doesn't just become another theory book that gets read and forgotten. By taking action after each chapter, you will be transformed into a productivity machine by the end of this journey.

Reasons for procrastination

So here's the million dollar question, why do we procrastinate? If we just knew the answer we would be able to solve it and achieve superhuman levels of productivity right?

Well unfortunately, the answer is not so simple. The reasons we procrastinate could be anything from having a traumatic event in the past that causes us to procrastinate doing something that might retrigger our traumas to feeling hungry and letting our hunger get the better of us. Given this broad spectrum, I've identified 3 key knights that when recruited will stack the odds in our favor against this hideous beast of procrastination. The three knights are

1. Clarity
2. Focus
3. Breaks

Clarity

The main reason we often procrastinate is that we don't know exactly what we are supposed to do or why we are doing it. Say for example you have an exam coming up but don't know how best to study or why bother studying. Or you want to start a new project but feel like there are too many things to do and again don't know where to start. This lack of clarity is often the cause we don't bother starting something new in the first place or we face a roadblock and give up.

This clarity will be solved by starting with the end in mind and then chunking it down from there, which we will be doing in the next chapters.

Focus

The second reason we procrastinate is that we lack focus. People often think of focus as some zen mode you enter to hone in 100% on your work, however focus is more like a renewable resource we get every day. You can think of focus as your energy levels, with times in the day when you have higher energy and higher levels of focus and times where you are depleted and have lower energy and focus. Typically, unless you are the vampire type that thrives at night, we start the day off in the morning with the most energy and focus. Then as we do more things that take up our energies and focus, this resource slowly wanes. Thus it is absolutely essential that we maximize the focus that we have.

Breaks

The final reason we procrastinate is we want a break but do not know when it is coming. Our body then tells us that it has enough and we take a break when we are supposed to be working or studying. I've come to realize that as much as I may want to work 24/7 on what I am passionate about, my body does not have the same enthusiasm I do and will quickly burn out from overwork.

You can think of our body like a phone. As it runs, the battery eventually dies out and if we run it all the way without taking time to charge it, the phone eventually dies. Our bodies work the same way. Without proper rest and recharging time, we eventually burn out and our bodies may react with diseases or sickness to make us take a break.

Lets dive into specific strategies to recruit these 3 knights into our arsenal against procrastination.

3

Timeline

The first knight we are recruiting comes with clarity. This comes with knowing what you want to achieve and then breaking it down into actionable steps for your year, month and days. Without clarity, whatever we do will just feel meaningless and unfulfilling as we don't know what we are working for. This leads to procrastination as we don't see any value in doing the work we are doing.

With clarity however, we are able to live life purposefully, taking actionables steps every day to get to our ultimate goals. This helps us stay more committed, motivated and focused on our work as we know the destination that we are headed to and how to get there.

The first step to gaining clarity is knowing what you want to achieve. This is your dream goal, in the area of finance that we will be focusing on, this could be your dream business of starting a gym or maybe your dream job of becoming a doctor. It could also be a material desire such as buying your dream car.

TIMELINE

Write this goal down on pen and paper along with the exact date you want to achieve it. Use the template 'I will be {dream business/job/material goal} by {year}'. Now read it out loud 3 times and really believe in your heart that you will achieve it. This gets the universe into motion to support you as it starts to notice your taking a step towards your goals.

Now count the number of years you have until your goal year that you have written. Write a roadmap of each year's goals from this year till your goal year and how you will get there. If you are unsure about it, do some research and come up with a timeline of how you will be getting there. You could ask a friend who already has the goal you want for advice or go online and search up how other people achieved what you want to achieve and get an idea from there of what you need to do.

After coming up with the yearly timeline, now you need to break down what you want to achieve this year into monthly goals. Again, if you need help do some research and ask the people who already have what you want to achieve or are further ahead than you for advice. Come up with your goal for each month and how to get there in a separate timeline for this year.

With your monthly timeline, look at your current month and start planning how you will get to your current month's goals this week. Break them down into actionables steps that you can start taking right this week to get you on track to reaching your monthly goals.

Finally with your goals this week, look at what you can start doing today to help you reach your weekly goals. Write down actionable steps that you can do today and over the next few days to help you reach your weekly goal and get your momentum flowing. By now you should have greatly increased the clarity you have on what to actually do to get you going towards your financial goals. This clarity will guide you along as we go into planning your day and the best way to do the steps that you have written.

Apply this by writing down your yearly timeline. Next, break this year's goal into months in your monthly timeline. Break this month's goals into weeks in your weekly timeline. Finally, break this month's goals into days by writing your daily timeline. We will see how to implement these daily goals in the next chapter.

4

Power Hour

Now that you have a clear idea of what your goals for this week are and clear actionable steps on how to get there, we will be going into something fun. I call this practice the power hour as this one hour will entirely determine the fate of your week ahead.

Now to employ the second knight of managing focus, prioritize this week's tasks according to which ones are most important at helping you reach your weekly goals. This prioritization will help you determine which high priority tasks should be done when your focus energy is at its peak and which tasks are not so important that can be done later in the day or night when your focus energy is lower.

Now for the Power Hour itself. Use one hour today to sit in front of your calendar(I recommend google calendar as it has nice color coding). Input all the actionable steps in order of priority you have for the week into your calendar, allocating the amount of time you estimate it will take to complete each task.

Put the more important high priority tasks when you estimate your focus energy is the highest, which is normally in the morning when you first wake up. If you are the vampire type who gets super into the zone at night, you could put these tasks at night when you will do your best work instead.

After putting the highest priority tasks, employ the third knight of breaks by giving yourself a short break, maybe 5 to 30 minutes right after your high priority task. This gives you time to recover and relax, allowing your focus energy to recover before your next tasks. Once you have inputted all your high priority tasks, allocate the other lower priority task when your focus energy is lower. This could be in the afternoon or night when you're having a food coma and your focus energy is temporarily lowered or in the day if you are the vampire type.

Congratulations, you have now planned your entire week ahead and know what needs to be done each and every day to reach your goals productively! Repeat this practice every week, taking some time to review what went well and what did not go so well to improve them for each future power hour.

This practice helps you get clarity in exactly what you need to do at each time to reach your goal. By taking each small step and clearing a task, your momentum will also build up making subsequent steps easier. With just this one practice, you are well on your way to walking the productivity path of success. Now the next step is actually doing the things you put in your calendar.

Apply this today by spending one hour to plan the next week ahead. Plan for next week's power hour as well. In the next chapter we will learn how to adjust this plan according to our priorities.

5

To Do Priorities

To ensure that you actually do what you were supposed to during the day, we need to again employ the first knight of clarity. I'm sure by now you're starting to become good friends with this wonderful handsome soldier. To ensure that our calendar is set properly, we will set a list of to do priorities the night before. Notice how it is not a to do lists as those lack an essential element; prioritization.

Before you go to bed tonight, look at your calendar of tasks that you planned for tomorrow. Take a small card or notebook and write down in order of priority what you need to finish tomorrow according to what you have planned. This is your 'To Do Priorities'. You may notice that one or more tasks that you put in for your maximized focusing time have been prioritized below another you put in a less focused time. Now is your chance to shift around your calendar for tomorrow so that the most important tasks are done at the timing where you are the most focused. As mentioned, this is usually first thing in the morning or at night for vampires.

Now that you have your list and your rearranged calendar, you are ready to go! As you go about your day the next day, have your To Do Priorities in front of you and tick each task off the lists as you finish them. This helps you again have clarity on which tasks you have completed and which tasks remain to be done.

At the end each day repeat the same process of looking at creating your next days 'To Do Priorities' and rearranging your calendar. If you have some high priority tasks that did not get completed that day, roll it over to the next day's To Do Priorities. For lower priority tasks that went undone, ask yourself whether it is really important right now. If it isn't, consider skipping it entirely. A lot of the time the reason we do not do it is because instinctively we know that it is not very important, which is why we procrastinate it into the next day.

By doing this practice, you will be able to keep track of what you are supposed to be doing every single day. This simple act alone of keeping track will cause your life to become more productive just based on the virtue of your attention being focused on what needs to be done.

Where attention flows, energy goes and results show. By placing your attention and focused intention on completing that task, it will instantly skyrocket the likelihood of you completing it.

Apply this by setting your To Do Priorities every night before you sleep, writing it in a notebook or card. Rearrange your calendar if you need to. Place these priorities somewhere where you will easily be able to see it when you are doing your priorities the next day.

Now that you have achieved clarity with Timeline, Power Hour and To Do Priorities, we will be moving on to the second knight of Focus.

6

Less is More

The secret to maintaining your focus is treating it like a resource. Many a time, people focus too much on time management instead of energy and focus management. The thing is, that's like trying to lose weight white only focusing on your diet and not exercising. Both are important! Similarly, as we have covered time management, now we will cover key skills in focus management to keep you razor focused on your tasks at hand.

With focus, less is more. Many times we have distractions cluttered all over our worktables. We have snacks, our phone buzzing, our stress ball calling out to us and we wonder why we get distracted so easily. The key is to simply remove all distractions that could take away from our focus so that we are able to focus on the things that truly matters the most to us.

Now I want you to look at your workspace and take note of what items you have on the table. Look at your phone, keyboard, notebook, pencil case and other items on the table and ask yourself this question, "Does this item help me to focus on my work?". If the answer is no, then remove it from your table and place it somewhere else. If the item is essential such as your mouse and keyboard, then by all means keep it. This short and simple exercise will easily help you remove distractions from your environment.

The most wondrous invention is your phone. Think about it, it can connect with millions of people around the globe! This also however means that your phone is your biggest distraction. This is often the number one servant of procrastination fighting against our knight of focus. It cannot be understated therefore how important it is to keep this servant of procrastination away from you while you are working or studying.

For myself, what I do is turn it to silent, put on airplane mode and put it out of sight and also more than an arm's length away from me when I work. This added difficulty in getting to it hinders procrastination from getting the better of your focus. Unless you absolutely need your phone for work, I highly recommend you turn it to silent or turn it off and put it far far away from you. If you want to go all out you might even put it in a locked safe or in a separate room.

Apply this by putting your phone out of sight and reach. Keep it silent or turned off the next time you want to focus on getting your tasks done.

7

You Are The Average Of Your 5 Closest Friends

I'm sure you have heard the saying 'Birds of a feather flock together'. This is especially true if you want to maintain your focus on your tasks and goals. It is often said that we are the average of our 5 closest friends and studies have even shown that we make similar incomes to the people we hang around with the closest.

The people we hang around have a tremendous impact on us, whether positive or negative. If we want to stay focused and committed to our goals and become more productive, it is thus imperative that we hang around people who have similar goals and motivations as us to cheer each other on. This helps to keep us focused on our goals and doing the things that really matter to us.

If you are trying to become a doctor, would you choose to hang out with your friend who is also studying and learning to take the test to apply for medical school? Or would you go out and party every night with your friends who are just seeking to have fun? The people that we hang around can either make or break us by empowering us with focus or becoming our biggest distractions.

How often have you been determined to spend the night studying or working on your new project when a friend casually invites you to hang out instead? Not that hanging out with others is necessarily bad as we all do need a social life, but who you hang out with either brings you towards or away from your goals.

Apply this by listing down your 5 closest friends and asking yourself 'Does this person support me in reaching my goals? Do they keep me focused on what matters to me?' If the answer is no, intentionally choose to spend less time with them and more time with those that help support you towards your goals.

8

The Grass is Greenest Where You Water It

Another common challenge that I myself face often is called the shiny object syndrome. It is where you are like a bird, going around and always scavenging for the newest shiny object, only to realize that when you come closer to it the object is as dirty as the other 10 that you collected.

Often, we hear the saying 'The grass is greener on the other side'. I find this to always be true no matter where you are in life. The current project you are on is facing some obstacles? The grass is greener on the new project your friend is starting, why not join him?

The main reason for this mentality is that we only see the obstacles in front of us. You may be facing a problem in your relationship now for example and feel tempted to go off with a new person you vibe with as you don't see any obstacles with them now. Obviously, should you choose to go with them, the obstacles will come along the way. Yet we do not see this and only focus on the difference between the obstacles we are facing now in this relationship and how pretty and obstacle free starting a new one will be. This is often why you see people jumping around from one relationship to another whenever an obstacle or argument occurs.

To counteract this mentally and keep your focus on your goals even through obstacles, it is imperative to realize that in truth the grass is not greenest on the other side. Instead, adopt the mindset that the grass is actually the greenest where you water it. Going back to the relationship example, it is clear that you may be facing some obstacles now. However, should you choose to push through with your partner and overcome it together, you will build more rapport with each other and end up closer than before. Compared to if you start a new relationship and run away from the obstacle, it is clear that by pushing through it you will be enjoying the fruits of a deeper, more intimate relationship. The grass is greenest where you water it.

This does not apply only to relationships but every aspect of life. In your work, business, health, spirituality and mental health. When you are set on a goal, keep your eyes laser focused on it without looking at what others are doing on the left or right and you will reach it at laser speed. Recruit the second knight of focus and take full advantage of all he has to offer.

Apply this when you see a shiny new object that tempts you away from your goals. Ask yourself 'Will this bring me closer or further from my goals? Is it aligned with what I truly desire?' These guiding questions will keep your eyes on the prize and prevent you from going after every shiny new opportunity that may pop up.

9

3 Breaths

In most of our lives, we live it unconsciously, just going through the motions of life without thinking much. This is why the majority of people are not really satisfied with their lives as they just go with the flow instead of pursuing their dreams and goals. As you're reading this book, it's clear you are not this majority as you are already improving every area of your productive life. Sometimes it feels like we are swimming against the tide that society is trying to shove down our throats. 'Get a good degree, a good job and you are set for life.' I hope by now you see how this lie has destroyed countless hopes and dreams.

In order to continue swimming upstream against this tide, we need to be present and increase our consciousness. There are many detailed meditations and guides on how to do this, but for the purpose of this book I will just share one small yet life transforming practice that will skyrocket your presence and help you focus better.

Before you start on a new task. Breathe out slowly and fully. As you breathe out, release all the thoughts and emotions you have of the past events that happened that day. As you breathe in, breathe in the life and energy to be excited, complete your task and bring you closer to your dreams. Think of how completing these tasks brings you one step closer to your dream life and get excited about it. Repeat this breathing out and then two more times and you should feel a rush of energy and excitement as you head into your next task.

This simple breathing technique will help you clear out all your past thoughts and emotions which may try to steal your focus as you do your task. It also energizes you and keeps you excited to finish the task ahead as you stay focused on the goals that you are accomplishing by doing that task. Although it seems really simple, just by taking a few conscious breaths every day before each task you would have drastically increased your consciousness and focus. This way you are also able to think better and be more creative doing your tasks as you do it consciously.

Apply this to your next tasks and take a deep breath out clearing your mind and emotions. Take a deep breath in breathing in life and excitement for the tasks ahead. Do this 3 times and get on your task with excitement and a clear mind!

We will move on to the final knight to recruit, our breaks.

10

You Are What You Eat

Have you ever heard the phrase 'You are what you eat'? While this is obviously not true in a literal sense as eating a steak doesn't make you become one, it is very true in the figurative sense. If for example, you went and watched violent movies and video games every day, along with being physically abused by your parents. There is a very high likelihood that you would become a violent person. Of course this may be quite an extreme example, but the point is that examining what we consume is very important.

This brings me to the third knight, breaks. What we do in our breaks can also take us either closer to or further away from your goals. If you are looking to lose weight, would you go and snack on a bag of potato chips every night while watching TV? In the same way, if you are looking to become a top salesperson, would you watch horror movies and learn how to scare children? It is hence imperative that we become hyper aware of every piece of media we consume daily and ask ourselves this question. 'Does this show/tiktok/game help bring me closer to my goals? Is it healthy for me?'

The best investment you could ever make is by investing in yourself and your education. This is probably why you bought this book and I'm sure you are getting tremendous value in applying these principles. Time is one of our most limited and valuable resources and like money, we can either choose to spend it or invest it. Instead of spending time during our breaks, why not choose to invest it in improving yourself and your skill sets? This helps accelerate the speed at which you will be going towards your goals and keeps your focus on your goals even doing your break times.

What I personally like to do during my breaks is listen to podcasts and read books that help me learn more about my industry or grow me personally. You can easily do this even while traveling on your drive to work, on the bus or on the train and even airplanes. This helps grow my knowledge of the field and figure out which aspects of my life I should be focusing on to reach the next level. I would recommend you start with listening to some podcasts and reading books about the industry you are in to get some insights into how to improve your business or work by learning from the best of the best.

Another great resource you could use is taking courses during your breaks. There are many amazing courses that could teach you everything from how to read faster to how to improve your sales pitch. Paid courses are also amazing as they have to compete with other paid courses in an open market, meaning only the best ones that provide the most value will come out on top. Of course, as with all things in life the course will not work unless you also do the work so keep that in mind when doing courses. With many online courses now to choose from as well, doing courses has never been more convenient and is a great way to accelerate your progress towards your goals even during your break times.

I also would recommend that as you go through these educational materials, do not just listen or read them and forget them. Take notes on each of them and at the end of the podcast or book chapter or course module, seek ways to apply what you just learned instantly. This way you instantly get the most value out of your education as you are already applying it. Theory alone won't improve your life, action creates the results that drive you towards your goals.

Now I want you to apply this and find one podcast, book or course that helps you towards achieving your goal. Buy it and start on it today! If you are short on money, go for the podcast option as they are usually cheaper or free.

11

Conclusion

Thank you for following me along this productive path. By implementing even one of these principles in your life, you will start to see your productivity skyrocket. If you choose to implement all of them, you will see yourself flying fast and accomplishing all your hopes and dreams! Go forth and achieve all that you set your mind to, you can do it!

If you found this book helpful, I would be deeply appreciative if you could leave a favorable review of this book on Amazon.

12

Resources

TechTarget. (n.d.). *Kaizen (continuous improvement)*. SearchERP. Retrieved June 22, 2024, from https://www.techtarget.com/searcherp/definition/kaizen-or-continuous-improvement#:~:text=Kaizen%20is%20a%20compound%20of,War%20II%20Japanese%20quality%20circles.

University of Michigan Youth Violence Prevention Center. (n.d.). *Video games and violent behavior*. Retrieved June 22, 2024, from https://yvpc.sph.umich.edu/video-games-influence-violent-behavior/#:~:text=Although%20playing%20violent%20video%20games,for%20more%20serious%20violent%20behavior.

Business Insider. (2012, July 9). *Jim Rohn: You're the average of the five people you spend the most time with*. Retrieved June 22, 2024, from https://www.businessinsider.com/jim-rohn-youre-the-average-of-the-five-people-you-spend-the-most-time-with-2012-7